BRAINCHIMP
EMPOWERING THE BRAINS OF BUDDING EINSTEINS

MW01092637

1 0 0
WORD
PROBLEMS

1ˢᵗ Grade Workbook For Ages 6 - 7

This book belongs to

For Exclusive Online Content And More Exercises Visit
WWW.BRAINCHIMP.COM

First Printing, 2012

Printed in the United States of America

ISBN-10: 1470054469
ISBN-13: 978-1470054465

Content Development
Shanthi Bhatnagar

Editing and Proofreading
Pency Lima M.

Illustrations and Cover Design
Selvarani R.

Concept and Book Design
Shireesh Bhatnagar

Order Online

WWW.BRAINCHIMP.COM

A
STRINAYS
PUBLICATION

www.strinays.com

Note To Parents And Teachers

This book (like other books in the BrainChimp series) aims to improve skills through better practice. It is a tool that can be used effectively in formal teaching scenarios and in self-paced learning.

Remember, consistency is key. Regular practice is essential to retain and master any set of skills. Better results will be achieved if there is a regular practice schedule. Daily practice is recommended when introducing new skills. Once a degree of proficiency is achieved, practice frequency can be changed to focus on retention of the newly acquired skills.

How To Use This Book

- Plan how many pages / problems the student is going to work on during one session.

- Plan how often the student is going to practice (Daily, Weekly, Twice Weekly, Thrice Weekly, etc.)

- The student must be allowed to practice in a calm environment free from distraction and noises.

- If the intention is to revisit the exercises again at a later date, take a copy of the page and let the student work on the copy.

- If used in a group setting like a classroom, encourage students to share their answers at the end of the exercise and engage in discussion on how they arrived at their answers.

- Refer to the answer key at the end of the book only after the exercises are completed for that session.

- Encourage students with positive reinforcement and ensure that the underlying concepts are revisited if the solutions are not accurate.

- Give students an opportunity to redo exercises that they did not get in the first attempt after the questions are reviewed and the concepts are reinforced.

Guidelines To Students

- Sit down comfortably at a table or desk to work on your exercises.

- Avoid any distractions like a running television.

- Read the question properly.

- Make sure you understand the question clearly. If not, read it again until you understand.

- Work out the problem in the space under the question.

- Write the answer in the space provided for answers.

- Review the answer to make sure it is correct.

- If answer is not correct, work out the problem again, erase the wrong answer and write the correct one.

- Stay focused till you finish all the questions or pages for that session.

- Get your teacher, tutor or parent to review your work and help you with any corrections.

- Pat yourself on the back. You've done a great job on your assignment. Your brain is now sharper than before.

1. Tracy has 7 chocolates and Vin has 5 chocolates. How many chocolates do they have in all?

They have _____ chocolates.

2. Anne collected 5 seashells on Saturday. On Sunday she collected some more seashells. Now she has a total of 9 seashells. How many seashells did Anne collect on Sunday?

Anne collected _____ seashells on Sunday.

5

3.   Tom went to the fruit market with his mom and bought 4 Apples, 6 Oranges, 3 Pears and 4 Potatoes. How many fruits did he buy?

Tom bought _____ fruits.

4.   David has $9. He bought a toy for $3. How much money will he be left with?

David will be left with _____ .

5.   There are 4 marbles in Basket A and 7 marbles in Basket B. How many marbles are there totally?

There are _____ marbles totally in both baskets.

6.   Grant is twice the age of Dan. If Grant is 18 years old, how old is Dan?

Dan is _____ years old.

7.   George has 5 apples. Josh has 9 apples more than George. How many apples does Josh have?

Josh has _____ apples.

8.   Matthew had 7 toy cars. He gave 2 toy cars to his friend Bryan. How many does Matthew have now?

Matthew has _____ toy cars now.

9. Hayley gave 6 stickers to Kaylee, 2 stickers to Bryan, 8 stickers to Greg. How many stickers did Hayley give away totally?

Hayley gave away _____ stickers totally.

10. Matthew sold 3 packets of popcorns for the cub scouts on Monday. He sold 6 packets on Tuesday and 9 packets on Wednesday. How many packets of popcorn did Matthew sell in all?

Matthew sold _____ packets of popcorn totally.

11. David has $3. He needs $9 more to buy his favorite book. What is the cost of the book?

Cost of the book is _____ .

12. Dan and Rick have the same amount of money. Rick bought snacks for $6. Now he has $7 left. How much money does Dan have?

Dan has _____ .

13.   Joe has 3 dimes and 3 quarters. How much money does he have?

Joe has _____ .

14.   Bob collected 5 seashells on Saturday. He collected 6 more seashells on Sunday. How many seashells did Bob collect totally?

Bob collected _____ seashells in all.

15. Josie has 6 marbles. Carla has 2 fewer marbles than Josie. How many marbles does Carla have?

Carla has _____ marbles.

16. Michael has 5 stickers in all. He has 3 more stickers than Andrew. How many stickers does Andrew have?

Andrew has _____ stickers.

12

17. Anna completed 9 questions in her workbook. Two of her answers were wrong. How many of her answers were correct?

Anna got _____ answers correct.

18. It is 4:00 pm. Hal has to go for soccer in another 2 hours. What time does his soccer practice start?

Hal's soccer practice starts at _____ .

19. Chris sold 4 packets of popcorn on Monday. He sold 12 packets on Tuesday. How many more packets of popcorn did he sell on Tuesday than on Monday?

Chris sold _____ packets more on Tuesday.

20. Richard had $14. He bought books for $3. How much money does Richard have now?

Richard now has _____ .

21. Dan borrowed 5 books from the library on Monday. He returned 3 books on Wednesday and borrowed 8 more books. How many books does Dan have now that he needs to return to the library?

Dan now has _____ books that he needs to return .

22. Josie has her dinner at 6:30 pm. She eats for half an hour. She reads her book for 1 hour. Then she goes to sleep. What time does she go to bed?

Josie goes to bed at _____ .

23. Victoria borrowed 7 books from library in 2 days. She borrowed 2 books on Monday. How many books did she borrow on Tuesday?

Victoria borrowed _____ books on Tuesday.

24. Trisha had 8 chocolates. She gave 4 chocolates to her brother. How many chocolates does she have now?

Trisha has _____ chocolates now.

16

25. Steve became the Secret Santa for 3 kids. He decided to buy 3 toys. Each toy cost him $10. How much did he spend on the toys?

Steve spent _____ on all the toys.

26. Rick has to arrange chairs in his class where parents are going to come to see the class play. He is expecting 20 parents. He has 6 chairs. How many more chairs does he need?

Rick needs _____ more chairs.

27. Pat's class had 15 kids. 3 more kids joined this month. How many kids are there in her class?

Pat's class has _____ kids now.

28. Janice is reading a book. She read 7 pages on Monday, 6 pages on Tuesday and 7 pages on Wednesday. How many pages did she complete by Wednesday?

Janice completed _____ pages by Wednesday.

29. Susie baked 15 cookies. Her friends came home and ate 9 cookies. How many cookies are remaining? She has to take 16 cookies to school the next day. How many more cookies does she have to bake?

_____ cookies are remaining.

Susie has to bake_____ more cookies.

30. Pat started his tennis game at 5:00 pm. The game is for 25 minutes. What time does his Tennis game end?

The Tennis game ends at_____ .

19

31. Rick loves to read books. He read 2 books on Monday, 2 on Tuesday, 3 on Wednesday, 1 on Thursday and 2 on Friday. On Saturday and Sunday he did not read any books but played outdoors instead. How many books did he read the entire week?

Rick read _____ books the entire week.

32. Hillary goes for soccer practice everyday. She plays every weekday (Monday, Tuesday, Wednesday, Thursday and Friday) for 20 minutes. How much time does she play soccer in a week?

Hillary played for _____ hours and _____ minutes totally.

20

33.   Jon has 2 nickels and 2 quarters. How much money does he have?

Jon has _____.

34.   Jack has 16 pencils and 3 erasers. His sister takes away 4 pencils and 1 eraser. How many pencils does Jack have now?

Jack has _____ pencils now.

35. Sally has 2 quarters, 2 nickels and 5 dimes. She wants to buy a toy that is $1. Does she have enough money to buy the toy?

Sally **has / does not have** enough money to buy the toy.

36. Kate has 6 blocks. She needs 18 blocks to make a shape. How many more blocks does she need?

Kate needs _____ more blocks.

37. A pizza has 8 slices. 3 slices were eaten. How many slices are remaining?

_____ slices are remaining.

38. Tom has 14 balloons. He buys 5 more balloons. How many balloons does he have now?

Tom has _____ balloons now.

39. There are 7 girls and 9 boys in the class. How many kids are there in the class?

There are _____ kids in the class.

40. Trisha went to a petting zoo and saw 6 sheep, 4 chickens, 3 goats and 3 ducks. How many animals and birds did she see totally?

Trisha saw _____ animals and birds totally.

41. For Halloween, Josh gave candies to the kids who came to his house. Of the kids who came to his house, 2 were dressed up as Smurfs, 3 were dressed up in Star Wars costumes, 5 were dressed up as ghosts, 3 as Dracula and 1 as Princess. How many kids came to his house? He gave each kid 2 candies. How many candies did he give?

_____ kids came to Josh's house.

Josh gave _____ candies in all to the kids.

42. You have 36 ¢. Can you figure out how many quarters, dimes and pennies will make 36 ¢?

_____ quarters, _____ dimes, _____ pennies.

43. The farmer's hen lays 2 eggs every day. How many eggs did she lay in 4 days?

The hen laid _____ eggs in 4 days.

44. Sue had 10 chocolates. She shared them equally between herself and her little sister. How many did each one get?

    Each sister got _____ chocolates.

45. Sally practiced every day for the music concert except Sunday. She practiced everyday for 20 minutes. How many hours did she practice in a week?

    Sally practiced for _____ hours a week.

46.   Hillary has 9 lollipops. She has 6 fewer than Sue. How many lollipops does Sue have?

Sue has _____ lollipops.

47.   Sam gets 1 point for every book he reads. He read 5 books in Week-1. He read 8 books in Week-2 and 7 books in Week-3. How many points did he get altogether?

Sam got _____ points in all.

48. Pat has a fish tank in her house. She has 6 Goldfishes, 7 Guppies and 4 Tetras. How many fishes does she have in her fish tank?

Pat has _____ fishes in her fish tank.

49. Greg has 4 pencils. Josh has 3 more than Greg. Joe has 2 less than Josh. How many pencils do they have altogether?

Greg, Josh and Joe have _____ pencils together.

Math Word Problems

50.   Tom gave away 4 toy cars, 5 toy trains and some toy planes. If he gave away 17 toys altogether how many toy planes did he give away?

Tom gave away _____ toy planes.

51.   Jenny has 3 different pictures. She wants to arrange them on her shelf. How many different ways can she arrange them?

Jenny can arrange the pictures in _____ different ways.

30

52. Wendy had saved $15 in her piggy bank. She bought a book for $4 and a Science Experiment kit for $7. How much money does she have in her piggy bank now?

Wendy has _____ in her piggy bank now.

53. Kate bought a toy for $7. She saw the same toy for $5 at another shop. If she had purchased the toy at the second shop how much would she have saved?

Kate would have saved _____.

54. Enay got $5 a week from his mom for taking food from home instead of eating at school cafeteria. At the end of 4 weeks, he decides to buy something nice for himself and his little sister. He buys a toy for $6 and a toy for his little sister for $5. How much does he have remaining with him?

Enay has _____ remaining with him.

55. Ethan and Josh go to a shop and spent $20 together. Ethan bought a toy for $8. How much did Josh spend?

Josh spent _____.

56. Josh got $50 from his mom for getting all A grades. He bought a fish tank for $8 and $5 for fish and $7 for fish food. How much money is he left with?

Josh is left with _____.

57. Ryan gets $10 a week for mowing his neighbor's lawn. He saves that money in his piggy bank. In how many weeks will he have $50 in his piggy bank?

Ryan will have $50 in his piggy bank in _____ weeks.

33

58. Linda got a doll for $7 and a Craft kit for $12. How much more did the Craft kit cost?

The craft kit cost _____ more than the doll.

59. Rick bought apples for $4 and had $13 remaining. How much money did he have in the beginning?

Rick had _____ apples in the beginning.

60. Rosy bought a toy pony for $7. If she gave the cashier $10, how much change did she get?

Rosy got _____ change back from the cashier.

61. Dan's mom bought a ball for $2 and a tennis racket for $12. She paid the cashier two 10 dollar bills. How much money did the cashier return to Dan's mom?

The cashier returned _____ to Dan's mom.

62. Trisha's tooth fairy gives her $3 for every tooth she loses. If she lost 5 teeth how much money would she get from the tooth fairy?

Trisha will get _____ from the tooth fairy

63. Ann's school has 5 grades. Each grade has 3 classrooms. How many classrooms are there in Ann's school?

There are _____ classrooms in Ann's school.

64. Greg eats an apple and a pear every day. How many fruits does he eat in 1 week?

Greg eats _____ fruits in 1 week.

65. North America and Central America have 24 countries and the South America has 12 countries. How many countries are more in North and Central America than South America?

North America and Central America together have _____ more countries than South America.

66. Diane has 6 strawberries. She has to divide the strawberries equally between herself, Rita and Cathy. How much will each one of them get?

Each one of them will get _____ strawberries.

67. Josh goes for a movie with 4 of his friends. The movie starts at 3:00 pm. The duration of movie is one hour and 30 minutes. What time does the movie end?

The movie ends at _____.

68. There are 22 students in Rick's class and Dave's class has 23 students. How many students are there totally?

There are _____ students in both classes together.

69. The Christmas tree has 25 wish balls. Chris's brothers David and Richard put 5 wish balls each. How many wish balls did Chris put on the Christmas tree?

Chris put _____ wish balls on the Christmas tree.

70. How many different ways can you mix and match 3 shirts and 2 pants?

   You can mix and match them in _____ ways.

71. Mars has 2 moons and Neptune has 13 moons. How many moons does Neptune have more than Mars?

   Neptune has _____ more moons than Mars.

72. Water, Soil, Sunlight and Carbon-Di-Oxide are needed for plants to survive and grow. Sarah pours 10 ounces of water for her plants every day. In 10 days, how many ounces of water did she use to water her plants?

Sarah used _____ ounces of water in 10 days.

73. An insect has 3 body parts and 6 legs. A beetle is an insect. There are 3 beetles in a jar. How many insect legs are there totally?

There are _____ insect legs totally.

74. It was 85 °F in the daytime. The temperature dropped to 70 °F in the night. How much did the temperature reduce from daytime to night?

The temperature reduced _____ °F.

75. A rain gauge measures how much rain falls. It rained on Monday and it showed 3 centimeters. On Tuesday the rain gauge showed 8 centimeters. How much more did it rain on Tuesday than Monday?

It rained _____ centimeters more on Tuesday than on Monday.

76. There are 4 seasons in a year – Spring, Summer, Fall and Winter. Trisha is 3 years old today. How many seasons has she seen so far?

Trisha has seen _____ seasons.

77. Sarah drinks milk every morning and night. She drinks 8 ounces both times. How many ounces of milk does she drink in 1 day?

Sarah drinks _____ of milk in one day.

43

78.   There are 15 chairs in a house. The legs of 4 chairs are broken. 12 guests arrive. How many of them will not have a chair to sit on?

_____ guests will not have a chair to sit on.

79.   It takes 2 people 2 days to dig a hole. How many days will it 4 people to dig a hole of the same size?

Four people can dig a hole of the same size in _____ days.

80. When water (a liquid) is cooled, it turns to ice (solid). 4 ounces of water makes 8 ice cubes. How many ice cubes can be made from 8 ounces of water?

_____ ice cubes can be made from 8 ounces of water.

81. For a Charity Drive, Andrew's class was supposed to bring 18 blankets. So far only 12 blankets have been collected. How many more blankets are needed?

_____ more blankets are needed for the charity drive.

82. Enay wanted to make a fruit salad with 5 apples, 3 oranges, 9 strawberries and 4 pears. How many fruits did he use in all for making the fruit salad?

Enay used_____ fruits to make the fruit salad.

83. 2 loaves of bread can feed 6 people. How many loaves of bread are needed to feed 18 people?

_____ loaves of bread are needed to feed 18 people.

84.   An endangered animal is a species which is close to becoming extinct. Bengal Tigers are endangered animals. Last year they had 12 Bengal Tigers in the National Zoo and this year they got 7 more. How many Bengal Tigers are in the National Zoo now?

       There are _____ Bengal Tigers in the national zoo now.

85.   Andy's house has 3 rooms and 1 bathroom. Each room has 3 lights and the bathroom has 1 light. How many lights are there in Andy's house?

       There are _____ lights in Andy's house.

86. Josh's class has two aquariums. One aquarium has fresh water fishes and the other one has tropical fishes. There are 6 tropical fishes and the total numbers of fishes in both tanks are 18. How many fresh water fishes are there?

There are _____ fresh water fishes.

87. Sally brought 20 cupcakes to her class. The students and the teacher ate 14 cupcakes. How many cupcakes is she left with?

Sally is left with _____ cupcakes.

88. In a room, there are 3 tables. Each table has 4 chairs. How many chairs are there in the room altogether?

There are _____ chairs in the room altogether.

89. 15 friends went for lunch. If 7 friends ordered Chicken Sandwich and the rest of the friends ordered Turkey Sandwich, how many of them ordered Turkey Sandwiches?

_____ of them ordered Turkey sandwiches.

90. There are 14 kids in Sarah's class and Sarah wants to give each kid 2 heart shaped candies for Valentine's Day. How many candies should she buy?

Sarah should buy _____ candies.

91. It is 3:00 pm. You have a piano class for 30 minutes and Gym class for 1 hour. You have a birthday party that starts at 5 pm. Do you have enough time to be ready for the party? How many minutes do you have to get ready for the party after the classes are over?

I **have / do not have** enough time to get ready for the party

I have _____ minutes to get ready for the party.

92. Your school starts at 8:00 am. You have 4 class periods of 1 hour each. Then you have your lunch. What time do you have your lunch?

I have lunch at _____ .

93. In a class of 23 kids, 16 kids scored more than 95 in the Math test. The remaining scored less than 95. How many kids scored less than 95?

_____ kids scored less than 95.

94. A pizza slice was divided into 4. You ate 2 pieces. Greg ate 1 piece and Dan ate the other piece. What fraction of the pizza did you eat?

I ate _____ of the Pizza.

95. George and Josh are twin brothers. Each earned 3 quarters and 5 dimes for doing chores at home. They would like to buy one race car that costs $2.00. Do they have enough money to buy one and how much money do they have in total?

☐ Yes they have enough money.
☐ No, They don't have enough money.
They have _____ in total.

96. Bob is 8 years older than Rob. If Rob is 6 years old, then how old is Bob?

Bob is _____ years old.

97. There are 6 guards guarding the North, 6 guarding the South, 6 the East and 6 the West palace gates. Enemy soldiers attacked the South and West gates and captured the guards. How many soldiers are remaining in the North and East palace gates totally?

_____ soldiers are remaining in the North and East gates.

98. Deforestation has caused many trees to be destroyed. This is not good for our environment. To help improve our environment, Dan's school started the project of planting trees. Every class planted 2 trees. There are 16 classes in Dan's school. How many trees did Dan's school plant altogether?

Dan's school planted _____ trees altogether.

99. To create an awareness of Recycling, every student was supposed to bring used cans. Tyler's class got 22 used cans and Sasha's class got 23 used cans. How many used cans did both the classes bring?

Both the classes brought _____ used cans altogether.

100. Sophia reads 5 books every week. In 4 weeks how many books would she have read?

Sophia would have read _____ books in 4 weeks.

1. Tracy has 7 chocolates and Vin has 5 chocolates. How many chocolates do they have in all?

    Traci has 7 chocolates

    Vin has 5 chocolates

    Total Number Of Chocolates
    $$= \text{Traci's chocolates} + \text{Vin's chocolates}$$

    $$= 7 + 5$$

    $$= 12$$

    They have _____12_____ chocolates.

2. Anne collected 5 seashells on Saturday. On Sunday she collected some more seashells. Now she has a total of 9 seashells. How many seashells did Anne collect on Sunday?

    Total Number Of Seashells Collected = 9

    Seashells Collected on Saturday = 5
    Seashells Collected On Sunday
    $$= \text{Total seashells} - \text{Collected on Saturday}$$
    $$= 9 - 5$$
    $$= 4$$

    Anne collected _____4_____ seashells on Sunday.

3. Tom went to the fruit market with his mom and bought 4 Apples, 6 Oranges, 3 Pears and 4 Potatoes. How many fruits did he buy?

        Apples Bought   =   4

        Oranges Bought   =   6

        Pears Bought   =   3

        Potatoes Bought   =   4

        Total Fruits Bought =   Apples + Oranges + Pears

                              =   4 + 6 + 3
                              =   13

      Tom bought   __13__   fruits.

4. David has $9. He bought a toy for $3. How much money will he be left with?

        David has   = $ 9

        Price Of Toy   = $ 3

        Money David will be left with

                =   Money that David has – Price Of Toy

                = $ 9 – $ 3

                = $ 6

      David has   __$ 6__   left with him.

5.   There are 4 marbles in Basket A and 7 marbles in Basket B. How many marbles are there totally?

       Basket A   has   4 marbles

       Basket B   has   7 marbles

       Total Number Of Marbles
            =   Number Of Marbles in Basket A   +
               Number Of Marbles in Basket B
            =   4   +   7
            =   11

       There are totally _____11_____ marbles.

6.   Grant is twice the age of Dan. If Grant is 18 years old, how old is Dan?

       Grant's age   =   18

       Grant's age is twice the age of Dan

       Dan's age   =   Half of 18

       Dan's age is   _9_

7.   George has 5 apples. Josh has 9 apples more than George. How many apples does Josh have?

   George has 5 apples

   Josh has 9 apples more than George

   Josh has   =   5 apples + 9 apples

               =   5   +   9

               =   14

   Josh has _____14_____ apples.

8.   Matthew had 7 toy cars. He gave 2 toy cars to his friend Bryan. How many does Matthew have now?

   Matthew had 7 toy cars

   Matthew gave Bryan 2 toy cars

   Matthew has   =   Toy cars Matthew had – Toy Cars
   given to Bryan

               =   7 – 2

               =   5

   Matthew has   5   toy cars now.

9. Hayley gave 6 stickers to Kaylee, 2 stickers to Bryan, 8 stickers to Greg. How many stickers did Hayley give away totally?

> Hayley gave Kaylee 6 stickers
>
> Hayley gave Bryan 2 stickers
>
> Hayley gave Greg 8 stickers
>
> Total stickers given = Stickers given to Kaylee +
>
> Stickers given to Bryan +
>
> Stickers given to Greg
>
> = 6 + 2 + 8
>
> = 16
>
> Hayley gave away   16   stickers.

10. Matthew sold 3 packets of popcorn for the cub scouts on Monday. He sold 6 packets on Tuesday and 9 packets on Wednesday. How many packets of popcorn did Matthew sell in all?

> Packets of popcorns sold on Monday   =   3
>
> Packets of popcorns sold on Tuesday   =   6
>
> Packets of popcorns sold on Wednesday   =   9
>
> Total Number of Packets sold = Packets sold on
>
> Monday + Packets sold on Tuesday + Packets sold on
>
> Wednesday
>
> = 3 + 6 + 9

60

$=$ 18

Matthew sold   __18__   packets of Cub Scout popcorns in all.

11. David has $3. He needs $9 more to buy his favorite book. What is the cost of the book?

    David has $3

    Money needed $=$ $9

    Cost Of Book $=$ Money that David has $+$
                              Money Needed

                   $=$ $3 $+$ $9

                   $=$ $12

    Cost of book is   __$12__

12. Dan and Rick have the same amount of money. Rick bought snacks for $6. Now he has $7 left. How much money does Dan have?

    Rick purchased snacks for $6
    Rick has a balance of $7
    In the beginning Rick had $6 + $7 $=$ $13

    Dan has what Rick had in the beginning.
    Dan has   __$13__ .

61

13.   Joe has 3 dimes and 3 quarters. How much money does he have?

   1 Dime   =   10 cents

   1 Quarter =   25 cents

   3 Dimes   =   10 cents + 10 cents + 10 cents = 30 cents

   3 Quarters =   25 cents + 25 cents + 25 cents = 75 cents

   Joe has   =   3 dimes + 3 quarters

              =   30 cents + 75 cents

Note: 100 cents make 1 dollar

              =   105 cents. (1 dollar and 5 cents)

Joe has   <u>105 cents.</u>

14.   Bob collected 5 seashells on Saturday. He collected 6 more seashells on Sunday. How many seashells did Bob collect totally?

   Seashells collected on Saturday =   5
   Seashells collected on Sunday   =   6
   Total seashells collected = Seashells collected on Saturday +
                              Seashells collected on Sunday

              =   5   +   6

              =   11 Seashells

Bob collected   <u>11</u>   seashells in all.

15. Josie has 6 marbles. Carla has 2 fewer marbles than Josie. How many marbles does Carla have?

Josie has 6 marbles

Carla has 2 fewer marbles than Josie

$$\text{Marbles Carla has} = \text{Marbles that Josie has} - 2$$

$$= 6 - 2$$

$$= 4$$

Carla has ___4___ marbles.

16. Michael has 5 stickers in all. He has 3 more stickers than Andrew. How many stickers does Andrew have?

Michael has 5 stickers. He has 3 more than Andrew.

3 Stickers + Stickers that Andrew has = 5 Stickers

$$\text{Stickers that Andrew has} = 5 - 3 = 2$$

Andrew has ___2___ stickers.

17. Anna completed 9 questions in her workbook. Two of her answers were wrong. How many of her answers were correct?

Total questions completed = 9

Number of Answers that were wrong = 2

Correct answers = Total questions completed –
Answers that were wrong

= 9 – 2

= 7

Anna got __7__ correct.

18. It is 4:00 pm. Hal has to go for soccer in another 2 hours. What time does his soccer practice start?

Current time = 4:00 pm

Duration until soccer starts = 2 hours.

Soccer practice start time = Current time +
Duration until soccer starts

= 4:00 pm + 2 hours

= 6:00 pm

Hal's soccer practice starts at _6:00 p.m._

19. Chris sold 4 packets of popcorn on Monday. He sold 12 packets on Tuesday. How many more packets of popcorn did he sell on Tuesday than on Monday?

Packets sold on Monday   =   4

Packets sold on Tuesday   =   12

Packets sold more on Tuesday
                =   Packets sold on Tuesday   —
                        Packets sold on Monday

                =   12   —   4

                =   8

Chris sold ___8___ packets more on Tuesday.

20. Richard had $14. He bought books for $3. How much money does Richard have now?

Richard had $14

Richard bought books for $3

Balance that Richard has   = $ 14   — $ 3

                = $ 11

Richard now has ___$ 11___.

21. Dan borrowed 5 books from the library on Monday. He returned 3 books on Wednesday and borrowed 8 more books. How many books does Dan have now that he needs to return to the library?

Number of books borrowed on Monday   =   5

Number of books borrowed on Wednesday =   8

Total Number of books borrowed

= Number of books borrowed on Monday(5) +

Number of books borrowed on Wednesday(8)

= 13 books

Number of books returned on Wednesday =   3

Books needed to be returned

=   Total borrowed books(13) −

Books returned on Wednesday (3)

= 10 books

Dan now has ___10___ books that he needs to return.

22. Josie has her dinner at 6:30 pm. She eats for half an hour. She reads her book for 1 hour. Then she goes to sleep. What time does she go to bed?

Dinner start time   =   6:30 pm

Time taken to eat   =   1/2 hour or 30 minutes

Josie reads book for   =   1 hour

Bed time   =   Dinner start time   +

Time taken to eat   +

Time taken for reading

=   8:00 pm

Josie goes to bed at __8:00 pm.__

23. Victoria borrowed 7 books from library in 2 days. She borrowed 2 books on Monday. How many books did she borrow on Tuesday?

Books borrowed in 2 days (Monday + Tuesday) = 7

Books borrowed on Monday = 2

Borrowed on Tuesday = Total books borrowed –
Books borrowed on Monday
= 7 – 2
= 5

Victoria borrowed ____5____ books on Tuesday.

24. Trisha had 8 chocolates. She gave 4 chocolates to her brother. How many chocolates does she have now?

Trisha had 8 chocolates

Trisha gave her brother 4 chocolates

After giving, Trisha has = 8 – 4

= 4

Trisha has ____4____ chocolates now.

25. Steve became the Secret Santa for 3 kids. He decided to buy 3 toys. Each toy cost him $10. How much did he spend on the toys?

Number of toys Steve has to buy   =   3

Price of a toy   = $ 10

Total Cost   = $10 + $10 + $10

   = $ 30

Steve spent   __$ 30__   on all the toys.

26. Rick has to arrange chairs in his class where parents are going to come to see the class play. He is expecting 20 parents. He has 6 chairs. How many more chairs does he need?

Parents expected to come   =   20

Chairs Available   =   6

Chairs needed   =   Parents coming – Chairs Available

   =   20 – 6

   =   14

Rick needs   __14__   more chairs.

27. Pat's class had 15 kids. 3 more kids joined this month. How many kids are there in her class?

    Kids in Pat's class before new kids joined   =   15

    Kids joined this month   =   3

    Total number of kids   =   Kids in Pat's class +

    Kids joined this month

    =   15   +   3

    =   18

    In Pat's class, there are   __18__   kids.

28. Janice is reading a book. She read 7 pages on Monday, 6 pages on Tuesday and 7 pages on Wednesday. How many pages did she complete by Wednesday?

    Pages read on Monday   =   7

    Pages read on Tuesday   =   6

    Pages read on Wednesday   =   7

    Total number of pages read   =   Pages read on Monday +

    Pages read on Tuesday +

    Pages read on Wednesday

    =   7 + 6 + 7

    =   20

    Janice completed   __20__   pages on Wednesday.

29. Susie baked 15 cookies. Her friends came home and ate 9 cookies. How many cookies are remaining? She has to take 16 cookies to school the next day. How many more cookies does she have to bake?

No. of cookies baked = 15

No. of cookies friends ate = 9

Remaining cookies = Cookies baked –

Cookies friends ate

= 15 – 9

= 6

Remaining cookies = 6 cookies

<u>6</u> cookies are remaining.

Cookies that Susie has to take to school = 16

Cookies Susie needs to bake

= Cookies Susie has to take to school –

Remaining cookies

= 16 – 6

= 10

Susie has to bake <u>10</u> more cookies.

30. Pat started his tennis game at 5:00 pm. The game is for 25 minutes. What time does his Tennis game end?

Tennis start time   =   5:00 pm
Game Duration   =   25 minutes

Time game ends   =   Start time +

Game Duration

=   5:25 pm

The Tennis game ends at   5:25 pm.

31. Rick loves to read books. He read 2 books on Monday, 2 on Tuesday, 3 on Wednesday, 1 on Thursday and 2 on Friday. On Saturday and Sunday he did not read any books but played outdoors instead. How many books did he read the entire week?

Books read on Monday   =   2
Books read on Tuesday   =   2
Books read on Wednesday   =   3
Books read on Thursday   =   1
Books read on Friday   =   2
Total Books read during the entire week

=   Sum of all the books read from
Monday through Friday
=   2 + 2 + 3 + 1 + 2
=   10

Rick read   10   books in entire week.

32.   Hillary goes for soccer practice everyday. She plays every
      weekday (Monday, Tuesday, Wednesday, Thursday and Friday)
      for 20 minutes. How much time does she play soccer in a week?

      There are 5 Weekdays (Monday, Tuesday, Wednesday,
                              Thursday and Friday)
      Practice time   =   20 minutes
      Total Practice Time   =   20 + 20 + 20 + 20 + 20
                             =   100 minutes
                                  (Note: 1 hour = 60 minutes)
                             =   1 hour 40 minutes

      Hillary played for __1__ hour and __40__ minutes totally.

33.   Jon has 2 nickels and 2 quarters. How much money does he have?

      2 nickels   =   5 cents   +   5 cents   = 10 cents

      2 quarters =   25 cents   +   25 cents   = 50 cents

      Jon has   =   2 nickels +   2 quarters

                  =   10 cents   +   50 cents

                  =   60 cents

      Jon has 60 cents.

34. Jack has 16 pencils and 3 erasers. His sister takes away 4 pencils and 1 eraser. How many pencils does Jack have now?

  Jack has 16 pencils and 3 erasers

  Jack's sister takes 4 pencils and 1 eraser

  Pencils Jack has after giving 4 to his sister

  $=\quad 16 - 4 \quad\quad = \quad 12$

  Jack has __12__ pencils now.

35. Sally has 2 quarters, 2 nickels and 5 dimes. She wants to buy a toy that is $1. Does she have enough money to buy the toy?

2 quarters	=	25 cents + 25 cents = 50 cents
2 nickels	=	5 cents + 5 cents = 10 cents
5 dimes	=	10 cents +10 cents +10 cents +
		10 cents + 10 cents
	=	50 cents
Sally has	=	50 cents + 10 cents + 50 cents
	=	110 cents (1 dollar and 10 cents)

  The price of the toy ($1) is less than what Sally has.

  Sally **has** enough money to buy the toy.

36. Kate has 6 blocks. She needs 18 blocks to make a shape. How many more blocks does she need?

   Kate has 6 blocks

   Kate needs 18 blocks

   Blocks needed   =   18 blocks – 6 blocks

                          =   12

   Kate needs ___12___ more blocks.

37. A pizza has 8 slices. 3 slices were eaten. How many slices are remaining?

   Total slices in the pizza   =   8 slices

   Slices eaten   =   3 slices

   Slices remaining   =   Total slices –
                                      Slices eaten

                                =   8 – 3

                                =   5

   ___5___ slices are remaining.

38. Tom has 14 balloons. He buys 5 more balloons. How many balloons does he have now?

Tom has 14 balloons

He buys 5 balloons

So, he has $\quad = \quad 14 + 5$

$\quad = \quad 19$

Tom has $\quad\underline{\quad19\quad}\quad$ balloons now.

39. There are 7 girls and 9 boys in the class. How many kids are there in the class?

Number of Girls $\quad = \quad 7$

Number of Boys $\quad = \quad 9$

Total Number of Kids $\quad = \quad$ Number of Girls + Number of Boys

$\quad = \quad 7 + 9$

$\quad = \quad 16$

There are $\quad\underline{\quad16\quad}\quad$ kids in the class.

40. Trisha went to a petting zoo and saw 6 sheep, 4 chickens, 3 goats and 3 ducks. How many animals and birds did she see totally?

Sheep seen	=	6
Chickens seen	=	4
Goats seen	=	3
Ducks seen	=	3
Total Animals and Birds seen	=	6 + 4 + 3 + 3
	=	16

Trisha saw ___16___ animals and birds totally.

41. For Halloween, Josh gave candies to the kids who came to his house. Of the kids who came to his house, 2 were dressed up as Smurfs, 3 were dressed up in Star Wars costumes, 5 were dressed up as ghosts, 3 as Dracula and 1 as Princess. How many kids came to his house? He gave each kid 2 candies. How many candies did he give?

Kids dressed up as Smurfs	=	2
Kids dressed in Star Wars costume	=	3
Kids dressed up as Ghosts	=	5
Kids dressed up as Dracula	=	3
Kids dressed up as Princesses	=	1

Kids who came to his house   = 2 + 3 + 5 + 3 + 1

_____14_____ kids came to Josh's house.

Each kid got 2 candies

Number of candies given   =   14 + 14   =   28

Josh gave _____28_____ candies to _____14_____ kids.

42. You have 36 ¢. Can you figure out how many quarters, dimes and pennies will make 36 ¢?

     1 Quarter   =   25 cents

     1 Dime   =   10 cents

     1 Penny   =   1 cent

     36 ¢   =   1 Quarter + 1 Dime + 1 Penny

               =   25 ¢ + 10 ¢ + 1 ¢

               =   36 ¢.

_____1_____ quarter, __1__ dime, __1__ penny.

43. The farmer's hen lays 2 eggs every day. How many eggs did she lay in 4 days?

   The hen lays 2 eggs in one day

   In 4 days the hen will lay $2 + 2 + 2 + 2$ $=$ 8

   The hen will lay __8__ eggs in 4 days.

44. Sue had 10 chocolates. She shared them equally between herself and her little sister. How many did each one get?

   Sue had 10 chocolates

   She has to share between herself and her little sister

   5   +   5 $=$ 10

   Each sister got __5__ chocolates.

45. Sally practiced every day for the music concert except Sunday. She practiced everyday for 20 minutes. How many hours did she practice in a week?

Practice time	$=$	20 minutes
Number of days	$=$	6 days
Hours practiced	$=$	$20 + 20 + 20 + 20 + 20 + 20$

(Note: 1 Hour = 60 Minutes)

$=$ 120 minutes (2 Hours)

Sally practiced for __2 hours__ a week.

46. Hillary has 9 lollipops. She has 6 fewer than Sue. How many lollipops does Sue have?

   Hillary has 9 lollipops

   Sue has 6 fewer than Hillary $=$ 9 + 6

   $=$ 15

   Sue has __15__ lollipops.

47. Sam gets 1 point for every book he reads. He read 5 books in Week-1. He read 8 books in Week-2 and 7 books in Week-3. How many points did get altogether?

   Books read in Week 1 $=$ 5

   Points got for Week 1 $=$ 5 (1 point for 1 book)

   Books read in Week 2 $=$ 8

   Points got for Week 2 $=$ 8 (1 point for 1 book)

   Books read in Week 3 $=$ 7

   Points got for Week 3 $=$ 7 (1 point for 1 book)

Total number of points   =   Points got for Week 1

+ Points got for Week 2

+ Points got for Week

=   5 + 8 + 7 =   20

Sam got   ___20___   points in all.

48. Pat has a fish tank in her house. She has 6 Goldfishes, 7 Guppies and 4 Tetras. How many fishes does she have in her fish tank?

Goldfishes   =   6

Guppies   =   7

Tetras   =   4

Total number of fishes   =   6 + 7 + 4 =   17

Pat has   ___17___   fishes in her fish tank.

49. Greg has 4 pencils. Josh has 3 more than Greg. Joe has 2 less than Josh. How many pencils do they have altogether?

Greg has 4 pencils

Josh has 3 more than Greg =   4   +   3

Josh has 7 pencils

Joe has 2 less than Josh   =   7 – 2

Joe has 5 pencils

Total number of pencils   =   Greg's pencils   +

$$\begin{aligned}
&\text{Josh's pencils } + \\
&\text{Joe's pencils} \\
= \quad & 4 + 7 + 5 \\
= \quad & 16
\end{aligned}$$

Greg, Josh and Joe have __16__ pencils together.

50. Tom gave away 4 toy cars, 5 toy trains and some toy planes. If he gave away 17 toys altogether how many toy planes did he give away?

Number of toy cars given away	=	4
Number of toy trains given away	=	5
Toy Cars + Toy trains given away	=	$4 + 5 = 9$
Total Number of Toys given away	=	17

(This includes toy cars, toy trains and toy planes)

Number of Toy planes given away	=	$17 - 9$
	=	8

Tom gave away __8__ toy planes

51.   Jenny has 3 different pictures. She wants to arrange them on her shelf. How many different ways can she arrange them?

She can arrange them in the following ways:

Picture 1, Picture 2, Picture 3

Picture 1, Picture 3, Picture 2

Picture 2, Picture 1, Picture 3

Picture 2, Picture 3, Picture 1

Picture 3, Picture 1, Picture 2

Picture 3, Picture 2, Picture 1

Jenny can arrange the picture in ___6___ ways.

52.   Wendy had saved $15 in her piggy bank. She bought a book for $4 and a Science Experiment kit for $7. How much money does she have in her piggy bank now?

Cost of Book	=	$ 4
Science Experiment kit	=	$ 7
Total money spent	=	Cost of Book + Science Experiment kit
	=	$ 4 + $ 7 = $ 11
Saved in piggy bank	=	$ 15
Balance	=	$ 15 – $ 11
	=	$ 4

Wendy has___$4___ in her piggy bank now.

53. Kate bought a toy for $7. She saw the same toy for $5 at another shop. If she had purchased the toy at the second shop how much would she have saved?

Kate purchased the toy for $7

Cost of the same toy in another shop is $ 5

She could have saved

$$= \quad \$ 7 - \$ 5$$

$$= \quad \$ 2$$

Kate would have saved $2

54. Enay got $5 a week from his mom for taking food from home instead of eating at school cafeteria. At the end of 4 weeks, he decides to buy something nice for himself and his little sister. He buys a toy for $6 and a toy for his little sister for $5. How much does he have remaining with him?

Money saved in a week	=	$5
In 4 weeks he will save $5 + $5 + $5 + $5	=	$20
Enay's toy price + Little sister toy price	=	$6 + $ 5
Amount spent on toys or expense	=	$ 11

Money remaining   =   His saving - expense
                    = $ 20 – $ 11 = $9

Enay has ____$ 9____ remaining with him.

55. Ethan and Josh go to a shop and spent $20 together. Ethan bought a toy for $8. How much did Josh spend?

Total money spent	=	$ 20
Cost of Ethan's toy	=	$ 8
Josh spent	=	Total money spent – Cost of Ethan's toy
	=	$ 20 – $ 8
	=	$ 12

Josh spent ___$ 12___ .

56. Josh got $50 from his mom for getting all A grades. He bought a fish tank for $8 and $5 for fish and $7 for fish food. How much money is he left with?

Cost of Fish tank	=	$ 8
Cost of Fish	=	$ 5
Cost of Fish food	=	$ 7
Total expense	=	Fish tank + Fish + Fish food
	=	$ 8 + $ 5 + $ 7 = $ 20
Balance	=	Total amount – Total expense
	=	$ 50 – $ 20
	=	$ 30

Josh is left with __$30__ .

57. Ryan gets $10 a week for mowing his neighbor's lawn. He saves that money in his piggy bank. In how many weeks will he have $50 in his piggy bank?

Ryan gets a week   = $10

In 2 weeks he will have $20
In 3 weeks he will have $30
In 4 weeks he will have $40
In 5 weeks he will have $50

Ryan will have $50 in his piggy bank in __5__ weeks.

58. Linda got a doll for $7 and a Craft kit for $12. How much more did the Craft kit cost?

Cost of Doll   = $7

Cost of Craft kit   = $12

Cost of Craft kit – Cost of Doll

                   = $12 – $7

                   = $5

The craft kit cost __$5__ more than the doll.

59. Rick bought apples for $4 and had $13 remaining. How much money did he have in the beginning?

Cost of apples is $4

After buying apples he has $13

Money he had in the beginning

$$= \quad \$4 \ + \ \$13$$

$$= \quad \$17$$

Rick had ___$17___ in the beginning.

60. Rosy bought a toy pony for $7. If she gave the cashier $10, how much change did she get?

Cost of toy pony	=	$7
Money Rosy gave the cashier	=	$10
Change that the cashier gave	=	$10 – $7
	=	$3

Rosy got ___$3___ change back from the cashier.

61. Dan's mom bought a ball for $2 and a tennis racket for $12. She paid the cashier two 10 dollar bills. How much money did the cashier return to Dan's mom?

Cost of Ball = $2

Cost of Tennis racket = $12

Total cost = $2 + $12 = $14

Money given to the cashier was two 10 dollar bills = $20

Change that cashier will give

= $20 – $14

= $6

The cashier returned ___$6___ to Dan's mom.

62. Trisha's tooth fairy gives her $3 for every tooth she loses. If she lost 5 teeth how much money will she get from the tooth fairy?

Tooth fairy gives $ 3 for 1 tooth.

For 5 teeth, Trisha will get $3 + $3 + $3 + $3 + $3

Trisha will get ___$ 15___ from the tooth fairy.

63. Ann's school has 5 grades. Each grade has 3 classrooms. How many classrooms are there in Ann's school?

Number of grades	=	5
Classrooms	=	3
Total classrooms	=	3 + 3 +3 + 3+3
	=	15

There are ___15___ classrooms in Ann's school.

64. Greg eats an apple and a pear every day. How many fruits does he eat in 1 week?

In 1 day Greg eats 1 apple and 1 pear.

Greg eats 2 fruits in 1 day

1 week has 7 days

Number of fruits he eats in 1 week

$$= 2 + 2 + 2 + 2 + 2 + 2 + 2$$

$$= 14$$

Greg eats ___14___ fruits in 1 week.

65. North America and Central America have 24 countries and the South America has 12 countries. How many countries are more in North and Central America than South America?

Countries in North and Central America   =   24

Countries in South America   =   12

Countries more in North and Central America than South America

$$= \quad 24 - 12$$

$$= \quad 12$$

North America and Central America together have <u>12</u> more countries than South America.

66. Diane has 6 strawberries. She has to divide the strawberries equally between herself, Rita and Cathy. How much will each one of them get?

Number of Strawberries   =   6

Number of kids   =   3

2 Strawberries for each kid equals 6 strawberries

Each one of them gets   <u>2</u>   strawberries.

67. Josh goes for a movie with 4 of his friends. The movie starts at 3:00 pm. The duration of movie is one hour and 30 minutes. What time does the movie end?

Movie start time   =   3:00 pm

Duration of movie   =   1 hour 30 minutes

Movie end time   =   Movie start time +
                             Duration of movie

                      =   3:00 pm + 1 hour 30 minutes

                      =   4:30 pm

The movie ends at 4:30 p.m.

68. There are 22 students in Rick's class and Dave's class has 23 students. How many students are there totally?

Students in Rick's class   =   22
Students in Dave's class   =   23
Total No. of students   =   Students in Rick's class +
                               Students in Dave's class

                           =   22
                               + 23
                              _____

                           =   45

There are totally ___45___ students.

90

69. The Christmas tree has 25 wish balls. Chris's brothers David and Richard put 5 wish balls each. How many wish balls did Chris put on the Christmas tree?

Wish balls in the Christmas tree	=	25
Wish balls that David put	=	5
Wish balls that Richard put	=	5
Wish balls that David and Richard put	=	10
Wish balls that Chris put		
	=	25 - 10
	=	15

Chris put __15__ wish balls on the Christmas tree.

70. How many different ways can you mix and match 3 shirts and 2 pants?

Shirt-1 → Pant-1   Shirt-1 → Pant-2
Shirt-2 → Pant-1   Shirt-2 → Pant-2
Shirt-3 → Pant-1   Shirt-3 → Pant-2

You can mix and match them in _6_ ways.

71. Mars has 2 moons and Neptune has 13 moons. How many moons does Neptune have more than Mars?

      Moons of Mars   =   2

      Moons of Neptune   =   13

      No. of moons Neptune has more than Mars

                         =   13 – 2

                         =   11

      Neptune has   __11__   moons more than Mars.

72. Water, Soil, Sunlight and Carbon-Di-Oxide are needed for plants to survive and grow. Sarah pours 10 ounces of water for her plants every day. In 10 days, how many ounces of water did she use to water her plants?

      In one day she pours 10 ounces of water

      In 10 days it will be

       =   10 + 10 + 10 + 10 + 10 + 10 + 10 + 10 + 10 + 10
       =   100

      Sarah used   __100__   ounces of water in 10 days.

92

73. An insect has 3 body parts and 6 legs. A beetle is an insect. There are 3 beetles in a jar. How many insect legs are there totally?

No. of legs a beetle has = 6

Number of beetles in the jar = 3

Total number of legs = 6 + 6 + 6

= 18

There are ___18___ insect legs totally.

74. It was 85 °F in the daytime. The temperature dropped to 70 °F in the night. How much did the temperature reduce from daytime to night?

Temperature at Day time = 85 °F

Temperature at Night time = 70 °F

Temperature that reduced from day time to night time

= 85 °F – 70 °F

= 15 °F

The temperature reduced ___15 °F___

75. A rain gauge measures how much rain falls. It rained on Monday and it showed 3 centimeters. On Tuesday the rain gauge showed 8 centimeters. How much more did it rain on Tuesday than Monday?

Rain gauge measurement on Monday $=$ 3 centimeters

Rain gauge measurement on Tuesday $=$ 8 centimeters

How much more did it rain on Tuesday

$=$ 8 centimeters $-$ 3 centimeters

$=$ 5 centimeters

It rained ___5___ centimeters more on Tuesday than on Monday.

76. There are 4 seasons in a year – Spring, Summer, Fall and Winter. Trisha is 3 years old today. How many seasons has she seen so far?

Seasons in a year $=$ 4
Number of years Trisha is $=$ 3
Number of seasons that Trisha has seen

$=$ 4 + 4 + 4

$=$ 12

Trisha has seen ___12___ seasons.

77. Sarah drinks milk every morning and night. She drinks 8 ounces both times. How many ounces of milk does she drink in 1 day?

No. of times Sarah drinks milk in 1 day $= 2$

Ounces of milk she drinks at 1 time $= 8$

Ounces of milk she will drink in 1 day $= 8 + 8$

$= 16$

Sarah drinks ___16___ ounces of milk in one day.

78. There are 15 chairs in a house. The legs of 4 chairs are broken. 12 guests arrive. How many of them will not have a chair to sit on?

Number of chairs $= 15$

Broken leg chairs $= 4$

Chairs that are good $= 15 - 4 = 11$

Number of guests $= 12$

Guests who will not have a chair are:

$= 12 - 11$

$= 1$

___1___ guest will not have a chair to sit on.

95

79. It takes 2 people 2 days to dig a hole. How many days will it 4 people to dig a hole of the same size?

2 people take 2 days to dig a hole

4 people is twice the number of people (2)
If people increase, it should take less time to dig the hole.
If people increase twice, the time taken should be halved.

Four people can dig a hole of the same size in ___1___ day.

80. When water (a liquid) is cooled, it turns to ice (solid). 4 ounces of water makes 8 ice cubes. How many ice cubes can be made from 8 ounces of water?

4 Ounces of water makes 8 Ice cubes

So 8 ounces of water should make double the number of ice cubes.

$$= \quad 8 + 8$$
$$= \quad 16$$

___16___ ice cubes can be made from 8 ounces of water.

81. For a Charity Drive, Andrew's class was supposed to bring 18 blankets. So far only 12 blankets have been collected. How many more blankets are needed?

Total blankets to be collected $=$ 18

Blankets collected so far $=$ 12

Blankets need to be collected $=$ 18 $-$ 12

$=$ 6

___6___ more blankets are needed for the charity drive.

82. Enay wanted to make a fruit salad with 5 apples, 3 oranges, 9 strawberries and 4 pears. How many fruits did he use in all for making the fruit salad?

Apples $=$ 5

Strawberries $=$ 9

Oranges $=$ 3

Pears $=$ 4

Total fruits

$=$ 5 + 9 + 3 + 4

$=$ 21

Enay used ___21___ fruits to make the fruit salad.

83. 2 loaves of bread can feed 6 people. How many loaves of bread are needed to feed 18 people?

        2 loaves of people can feed 6 people.
        18 people are three groups with 6 in each. It is thrice the number of people.

        What is thrice the value of 2 loaves of bread?
        It is $2 + 2 + 2 = 6$

        __6__ loaves of bread are needed to feed 18 people.

84. An endangered animal is a species which is close to becoming extinct. Bengal Tigers are endangered animals. Last year they had 12 Bengal Tigers in the National Zoo and this year they got 7 more. How many Bengal Tigers are in the National Zoo now?

        Last year there were 12 Bengal Tigers in the National Zoo.

        This year they got 7 more Bengal Tigers in the Zoo.

        Total number of Bengal tigers in the Zoo

$$= \quad 12 + 7$$

$$= \quad 19$$

        There are __19__ Bengal Tigers in the National Zoo now.

85. Andy's house has 3 rooms and 1 bathroom. Each room has 3 lights and the bathroom has 1 light. How many lights are there in Andy's house?

Total rooms	=	3
Bathroom	=	1
Number of Lights in 1 room	=	3
Number of lights in all rooms	=	$3 + 3 + 3 = 9$
Number of lights in bathroom	=	1
Total number of lights	=	$9 + 1 = 10$

There are __10__ lights in Andy's house.

86. Josh's class has two aquariums. One aquarium has fresh water fishes and the other one has tropical fishes. There are 6 tropical fishes and the total numbers of fishes in both tanks are 18. How many fresh water fishes are there?

Total number of fishes	=	18
Total number of tropical fishes	=	6

Total number of fresh water fishes   =
Total number of Fishes −
Total number of tropical fishes
                    = $18 - 6$
                    =   12

There are __12__ fresh water fishes.

87. Sally brought 20 cupcakes to her class. The students and the teacher ate 14 cupcakes. How many cupcakes is she left with?

Total cupcakes brought $=$ 20

Students and teachers ate $=$ 14 cupcake

Remaining cupcakes $=$ Total cupcakes brought $-$ No. of cupcakes eaten

$=$ 20 $-$ 14

$=$ 6

Sally is left with __6__ cupcakes.

88. In a room, there are 3 tables. Each table has 4 chairs. How many chairs are there in the room altogether?

No. of tables $=$ 3

No. of chairs for 1 table $=$ 4

Total no. of chairs $=$ 4 + 4 + 4

$=$ 12

There are __12__ chairs in the room altogether.

100

89.   15 friends went for lunch. If 7 friends ordered Chicken Sandwiches and the rest of the friends ordered Turkey Sandwiches. How many of them ordered Turkey Sandwiches?

Number of friends who went to lunch	=	15 friends
Chicken Sandwiches ordered	=	7 friends
Turkey Sandwiches ordered	=	15 – 7
	=	8

 _8_ friends ordered chicken sandwiches.

90.   There are 14 kids in Sarah's class and Sarah wants to give each kid 2 heart shaped candies for Valentine's Day. How many candies should she buy?

Kids in Sarah's class	=	14
Candies for each kid	=	2
Candies for all the kids		
	=	14 + 14
	=	28

Sarah buys _28_ candies.

91. It is 3:00 pm. You have a piano class for 30 minutes and Gym class for 1 hour. You have a birthday party that starts at 5 pm. Do you have enough time to be ready for the party? How many minutes do you have to get ready for the party after the classes are over?

Current time	=	3:00 p.m.
Duration for Piano class	=	30 minutes
Time after going for piano class	=	3:30 p.m.
Duration for Gym class	=	1 hour
Time after going for gym class	=	4:30 p.m.

Birthday party starts at 5:00 pm. I will have 30 minutes left.

I **have** enough time to get ready for the party

I have **30** minutes to get ready for the party.

92. Your school starts at 8:00 am. You have 4 class periods of 1 hour each. Then you have your lunch. What time do you have your lunch?

School start time	=	8:00 am
Duration of each class period	=	1 hour
For 4 class periods it will be	=	4 hours
Time 4 hours after 8:00 am will be	=	8:00 am + 4 hours
	=	12:00 pm

I have lunch at 12:00 p.m.

93. In a class of 23 kids, 16 kids scored more than 95 in the Math test. The remaining scored less than 95. How many kids scored less than 95?

      Total no. of kids in class   =   23

      No. of kids got more than 95   =   16

      Kids who scored less than 95   =

            Total no. of kids –
            No. of kids who scored more than 95

            =   23 – 16

            =   7

      ___7___ kids scored less than 95.

94. A pizza slice was divided into 4. You ate 2 pieces. Greg ate 1 piece and Dan ate the other piece. What fraction of the pizza did you eat?

      No. of pizza slices   =   4

      No. of slices you ate =   2

      I ate __2/4 or ½__ of the Pizza.

95. George and Josh are twin brothers. Each earned 3 quarters and 5 dimes for doing chores at home. They would like to buy one race car that costs $2.00. Do they have enough money to buy one and how much money do they have in total?

Each of them earned

3 quarters	=	25¢ + 25¢ + 25¢ = 75¢
and 5 dimes	=	10¢ + 10¢ + 10¢ + 10¢ + 10¢
	=	50¢
	=	75¢ + 50¢ = 1 dollar 25¢
George's money	=	1 dollar 25 cents
Josh's money	=	1 dollar 25 cents
Total money earned	=	1 dollar 25¢ + 1 dollar 25 ¢
	=	2 dollar 50¢
Cost of race car	=	$ 2.00

__Yes__ They have enough money.
They have __$2. 50__ in total.

96. Bob is 8 years older than Rob. If Rob is 6 years old, then how old is Bob?

Rob's age = 6 years

Bob's age = Rob's age + 8 years

$\qquad$ = 6 + 8

$\qquad$ = 14

Bob is __14__ years old.

97. There are 6 guards guarding the North, 6 guarding the South, 6 the East and 6 the West palace gates. Enemy soldiers attacked the South and West gates and captured the guards. How many total guards are remaining in the North and East palace gates?

Total no. of guards guarding	=	Guards in North +
		Guards in South +
		Guards in East +
		Guards in West
	=	6 + 6 + 6 + 6
	=	24
Number of guards attacked	=	6 + 6
	=	12
Guards remaining	=	24 – 12
	=	12

___12___ soldiers are remaining in the North and East gates.

98. Deforestation has caused many trees to be destroyed. This is not good for our environment. To help improve our environment, Dan's school started the project of planting trees. Every class planted 2 trees. There are 16 classes in Dan's school. How many trees in Dan's school plant altogether?

Number of classes	=	16		
Each class planted	=	2 trees		
Number of trees planted	=	16 + 16	=	32

Dan's school planted ___32___ trees altogether.

99. To create an awareness of Recycling, every student was supposed to bring used cans. Tyler's class got 22 used cans and Sasha's class got 23 used cans. How many used cans did both the classes bring?

Tyler's class got 22 cans

Sasha's class got 23 cans

Total cans brought   =   Cans brought in Tyler's class +
                            Cans brought in Sasha's class

                     =   22 + 23

                     =   45

Both the classes brought __45__ used cans altogether.

100. Sophia reads 5 books every week. In 4 weeks how many books would she have read?

Sophia reads 5 books in 1 week.

Number of weeks   =   4

In 4 weeks she will read $5 + 5 + 5 + 5 = 20$

Sophia would have read __20__ books in 4 weeks.

Made in the USA
Lexington, KY
11 May 2016